Cambridge ICT Starters

Next Steps Stage 1

Third Edition

Jill Jesson and Graham Peacock

CAMBRIDGE
UNIVERSITY PRESS

CAMBRIDGE
UNIVERSITY PRESS

4381/4 Ansari Road, Daryaganj, Delhi 110002, India

Cambridge University Press is part of the University of Cambridge.

It furthers the University's mission by disseminating knowledge in the pursuit of education, learning and research at the highest international levels of excellence.

www.cambridge.org
Information on this title: www.cambridge.org/9781107625068

First published 2003
Second edition 2005
Third edition 2013

Printed in India by Shree Maitrey Printech Pvt. Ltd., Noida

A catalogue record for this publication is available from the British Library

ISBN 978-1-107-62506-8 Paperback

Additional resources for this publication at www.cambridgeindia.org

Cambridge University Press has no responsibility for the persistence or accuracy of URLs for external or third-party internet websites referred to in this publication, and does not guarantee that any content on such websites is, or will remain, accurate or appropriate. Information regarding prices, travel timetables, and other factual information given in this work is correct at the time of first printing but Cambridge University Press does not guarantee the accuracy of such information thereafter.

....

....

Every effort has been made to trace the owners of copyright material included in this book. The publishers would be grateful for any omissions brought to their notice for acknowledgement in future editions of the book.

Introduction

Cambridge ICT Starters: Next Steps, Stage 1 has been written to support learners who are following the Cambridge ICT Starters syllabus. It follows the syllabus closely and provides full coverage of all the modules. The sections of the book correspond to the modules and follow the order in which the modules appear in the syllabus. The book builds on creating, amending and refining documents; designing cards and posters; producing, amending and interpreting spreadsheets and graphs; and exploring, modifying and interpreting databases.

The book provides learners and their helpers with:

- examples of activities to do
- exercises for practice
- instruction in using their computers
- optional extension and challenge activities

It is designed for use in the classroom with coaching from trained teachers. Where possible the work has been set in real situations where the computer will be of direct use. The activities are fairly sophisticated yet simple enough to be followed by adults as well as children!

Some exercises require the learners to open prepared files for editing. These files are available to teachers on www.cambridgeindia.org website. The website provides useful graphics and templates for creating pictograms. Some pictures and text files are also included to help young learners so that they can learn editing without first creating the files required.

The activities in this book use Windows 7, Microsoft Office 2007 software and Paint. However, the syllabus does not specify any particular type of software in order to meet the learning objectives.

Please note that when learners view the screen shots contained in this book on their computer screens, all the type will be clearly legible.

Contents

Module 1
Exploring Documents

Learning Objectives

	Student is able to:	Pass/Merit
1	Create and amend a text document	P
2	Amend text for a specific audience	P
3	Add images or other objects to a document	P
4	Refine and organise the layout of a document for a specific audience	M
5	Evaluate a finished document	M

1.1 New document

Word wrap

- Load Microsoft Word [W] Microsoft Office Word 2007 .
- Start with a blank new document.
- Type the sentences on the right. When you reach the end of a line, just keep typing, don't tap [←Enter].
- Word will automatically **wrap** the text to the next line.
- Click [≡] before you type to ensure that the text you are going to type is **justified**.

Mr Mohammad Salleh is a very successful businessman. Today, he is the manager of two companies and Chairman of six other companies.

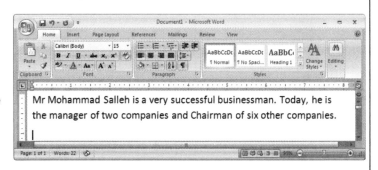

Paragraph break

- Tap [←Enter] once to force a line break.
- Tap [←Enter] twice. This will insert 2 blank lines.
- Tap [Delete] to remove the line break.
- Tap [←Enter] twice to get a paragraph break.

  Tap [Delete] twice to remove the paragraph break.
- Type the next two paragraphs with a break between each of the three paragraphs.

Mr Mohammad Salleh came from a very poor family. His father could hardly give him any money to buy books. Mr Mohammad Salleh therefore worked in a coffee shop in the afternoon. He studied very hard.

After graduating as a lawyer, Mr Mohammad Salleh could not find a job as a lawyer, so he worked as a salesman.

Paragraph alignment

- Place the cursor somewhere in the first paragraph.
- Click [≡].
- This will align the whole paragraph to the centre.
- Place the cursor somewhere in the second paragraph.
- Click [≡].
- This will align the whole paragraph to the right.

- Place the cursor somewhere in the third paragraph.
- Click [≡].
- This will align the whole paragraph to the left.
- Adjust the alignment so that the whole passage is justified.
- Save your work as MSalleh.

1.2 Selecting and changing

Select words

- Click  to start with a new blank page.
- Type the following sentences:

  She has two cute pets.

  He has eight small animals in his family.

  I have five big cats in my house.
- You must select a word before you can change it.
- You can select a word using the mouse in three ways:
  - Double-click it.
  - Click at the beginning and drag.
  - Click at the end and drag.

Select a word and delete it

- You can delete a selected word in three ways:
  - Click on ✂ to cut the word.
  - Tap on Backspace ←.
  - Tap on Delete.
- Select the word cute and click ✂.
- Select the word small and tap Backspace ←.
- Select the word big and tap Delete.

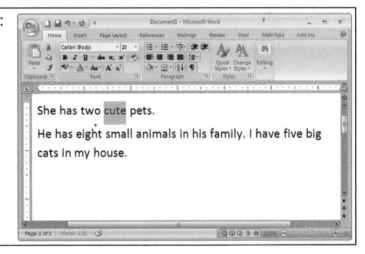

Change a word

- Select the word two.
- Type the word three.
- The new word replaces the selected word.
- Select and change the word eight to ten.
- Select and change the word I to We.
- Select and change the word my to our.

The new word replaces the selected word.

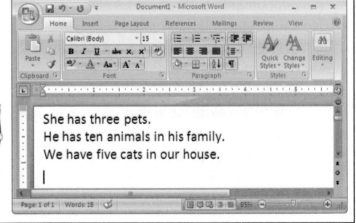

1.3 Cut and paste

Moving text

- Type these instructions about heating some beans. They are in the wrong order.

  Put the beans in the pan.
  Open the tin.
  Put the hot beans on the plate.
  Get the tin from the cupboard.

- Let us put the instructions in the correct order using cut ✂ and paste 📋.

- Highlight the last sentence Get the tin from the cupboard.

- Click ✂.

- Click in front of the first line and click 📋.

- Highlight the next line Put the beans in the pan.

- Click ✂.

- Click in front of the line Put the hot beans on the plate.

- Click 📋.

- If the lines are joined together, click in front of the first character of the second line and tap ⏎ Enter to force the second line down.

  Get the tin from the cupboard.
  Open the tin.
  Put the beans in the pan.
  Put the hot beans on the plate.

Making tea

- Type these instructions.

  Add hot water.
  Pour the tea.
  Put the tea in the pot.
  Drink it.

- Now put them in the correct order.

Insert the instruction Add the sugar in a sensible place in the list.

Revision exercise

- Click 📂 and open the file mylist.
- Highlight all the sentences.
- Click 📋 to copy all the sentences.
- Click ☐ to open a new blank document.
- Click 📋 to paste all the sentences into this new document.
- Now make the following changes:
  - Correct the spelling mistakes poool to pool; couter to counter.
  - Replace five with twenty.
  - Delete the extra word your.
- Click 💾 to save the document as mylist2.
- Use **cut and paste** to put the list in the correct order.
- Save the corrected version as mylist3.

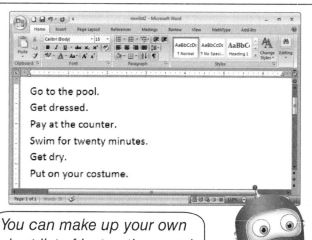

You can make up your own short list of instructions, and put them in the wrong order. Challenge your friend to put the list back in the correct order.

1.4 Spellchecker

Spelling – change

- Click 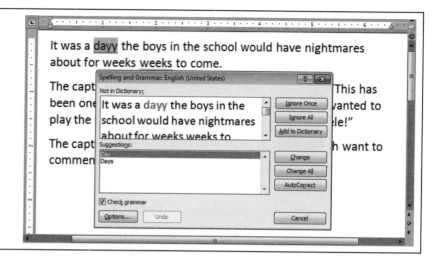 and open the file GreatVictory.
- Click to start checking for spelling errors.
- A mistake dayy identified by the spellchecker is shown in red.
- The spellchecker suggests day as the replacement.
- Click Change to accept the suggestion.

Spelling – delete

- The spellchecker will continue to check the file GreatVictory for more mistakes.
- It has found a repeated word weeks.
- Click Delete to delete the repeated word.

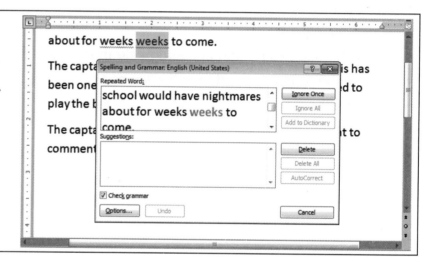

Spelling – ignore

- The spellchecker has found another word that is not in its dictionary.
- Kumang is the name of a girl. In this case it is spelt correctly and need not be changed.
- Click Ignore All to keep it.
- Continue to check for other mistakes.
- When you have finished with the rest of the corrections, save the checked file as GirlsVictory.

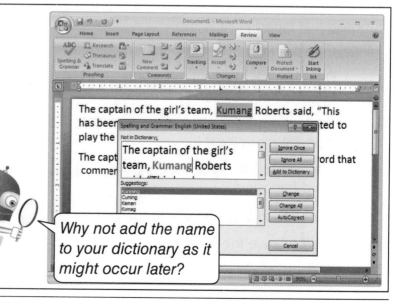

Why not add the name to your dictionary as it might occur later?

1.5 Long documents

New document

- Load Microsoft Word [W].
- Start with a new document.
- Type the following text. Tap [Tab ⇆] to begin the first indent.
- Don't tap the [← Enter] key at the end of the line. Let Microsoft Word do the automatic word wrapping for you, unless you are starting a new paragraph.

  Imported fruits

  A lot of Malaysians like to eat fruits. In fact Malaysia produces a seemingly endless variety of tropical fruits. Bananas, papayas, pineapples and watermelons are available through the year. Some other fruits like rambutans, durians, mangosteens and langsat are only seasonal.

- Save the text as fruits.
- Open the file imported fruits.
- Copy the last two paragraphs and paste them below the paragraph that you have just typed.
- Delete the repeated word to in the second paragraph.
- Change the first letter of they, t to capital letter T.
- Replace the word medical with medicinal.
- Read through the whole text to find out whether there are any other mistakes. If there are, correct them.
- Use the spellchecker to ensure that there are no other spelling mistakes.
- Save your work as fruits1.

Change the title

- Make the following adjustments to the text you have just typed.
- Change the title:
  - Double-click to select the word Imported in the title.
  - While the word is still highlighted type Eat more local.
  - The words Eat more local replace the word Imported.
  - Click ≡ to align the title to the centre.
- Click 💾 to save the file again.

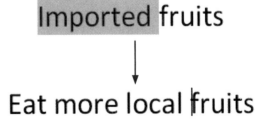

You don't have to delete the word Imported.

Inserting missing words

- Insert the word imported.
  - ○ Click the cursor I in front of the word fruits in the first sentence of the first paragraph.
  - ○ Type imported.
  - ○ Tap the space bar once.
- Insert the word most.
  - ○ Click the cursor I in front of the words orchard farmers in the second sentence of the second paragraph.
  - ○ Type most.
  - ○ Tap the space bar once.
- Insert the word local.
  - ○ Click the cursor I in front of the word fruits in the first sentence of the third paragraph.
  - ○ Type local.
  - ○ Tap the space bar once.

Replacing words

- Replace the word through with throughout in the sentence Bananas, papayas, pineapples and watermelons are available <u>through</u> the year.
  - ○ Double-click on the word through.
  - ○ Type throughout.
- Replace the word period with time in the sentence It is also a profitable <u>period</u> for most orchard farmers.
  - ○ Double-click on the word period.
  - ○ Type time.

Move a paragraph

- Move the second paragraph to become the third paragraph.
  - ○ Click in front of the first word of the second paragraph.
  - ○ Hold down the mouse and drag to highlight the whole paragraph.
  - ○ Click ✄.
  - ○ Click the cursor I at the end of the last paragraph.
  - ○ Tap ⏎Enter twice.
  - ○ Click 📋.
- Save the amended text as fruits2.

After highlighting the paragraph, you can drag the highlighted sentences to the end of the third paragraph, and then drop it by releasing the mouse button.

1.6 Amend text for a specific audience

Changing font style

- Open the file fruits2 that you saved in the previous exercise.
- Change the font style of the title:
  - Highlight the title.
  - Click ▾ of Calibri (Body) ▾ to get a drop-down list of font styles.
  - Drag the scroll bar up and down until you find the font style .
  - Click ⊤ Impact .
- You can change to another font style if you cannot find ⊤ Impact . Choose one that makes the title stand out to attract the attention of your audience.

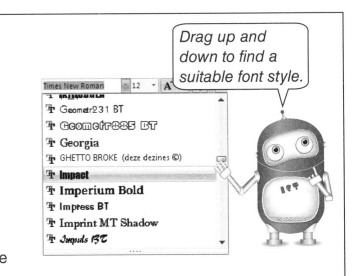

Drag up and down to find a suitable font style.

Changing font size

- Change the font size of the title:
  - Highlight the title.
  - Click on the option for font sizes.
  - Click 26 to select it as the desired font size.
  - You can choose other sizes. The larger the number, the larger the font size.
  - We normally make the title bigger than the rest of the text to attract our targeted audience.
- Save the file as fruits3.

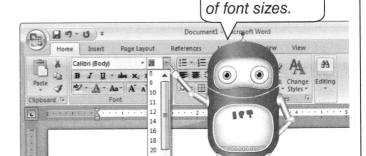

Click here to get a drop-down list of font sizes.

Changing font colour

- Change the colour of the title:
  - Highlight the title again.
  - Click **A**▾ to get a table of colours.
  - Click on the red colour.
  - You can also choose other colours for the title.
- Changing the font colour will make the title more eye-catching and thus help to attract the target audience.
- Click 💾 to save the file.

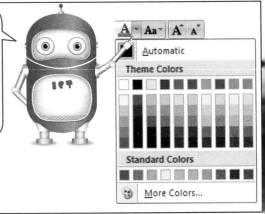

Click here to get a table of colours. Click on the colour desired to select it.

1.7 Inserting images

Learning Objective: 3

Add an image

- Open the file fruits3.
- Click to place the cursor I at the blank line between the title and the first paragraph.
- Tap [←Enter] once to insert a blank line.
- Click on Insert tab.
- Click [Picture].
- Select the appropriate picture of fruits (e.g. MsiaFruits.jpg).
- Click [Insert ▼].
- Tap [←Enter] once to insert a blank line.
- Save your work as fruits4.

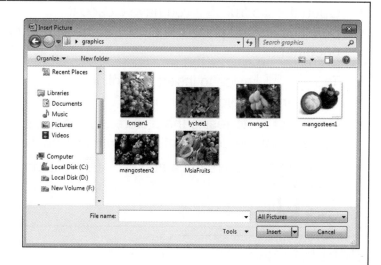

Resizing the picture

- Click somewhere in the picture.
- Resize the picture to an appropriate size by dragging the resize handles at the edge of the picture.
- When you bring the mouse pointer on top of the handle, it will change its shape from ⬉ to a resize pointer.
- With ⟺ you resize the picture horizontally.
- With ↕ you resize the picture vertically.
- With ⬂ or ⬈ you resize the picture diagonally.
- Only ⬂ and ⬈ will resize the picture proportionally without distorting the picture.
- Dragging away from the picture will increase its size.
- Dragging towards the picture will reduce its size.
- Click 💾 to save your work after the picture is resized.

Drag in the diagonal direction away from the picture to enlarge it proportionally.

Alignment of picture

- At this stage, you can only align the picture using the paragraph alignment tool.
- Click on the picture once.
- Click ≣, the picture is aligned left.

- Click ≣, the picture is aligned at the centre.
- Click ≣, the picture is aligned right.
- Align your picture at the centre and save your work as fruits5.

Inserting more pictures

- Open the file fruits5 if you have closed it.
- Scroll down and place the cursor at the end of the document.
- Tap ⬅Enter twice to insert 2 blank lines.
- Insert another picture durian.jpg.
- Use ↖ or ↗ to resize the picture to an appropriate size so that the document is still within 1 page.
- Click on the picture once and click ≡ to align at the centre.
- Click 💾 to save the file.

durian.jpg

Delicious!

Print preview

- Click 🔵, hover over 🖨 Print to see 🔍.
- A print preview is displayed. We use this feature to check the output layout without actually printing it. We can save printing costs this way.
- If you have only one printer connected to your PC, you can click 🖨 to print a copy, using the default print setting.
- Click 📖 if you want to have full screen view.
- Drag 🔽 on the right of 51% ▲▼ to zoom in by increasing the figure shown or zoom out by decreasing the figure.
- You can also select ☑ Magnifier to get a magnifier.
- Click on the preview display to magnify the view or click again to return to the normal preview display.
- Click ❎ Close Print Preview to close the preview mode.

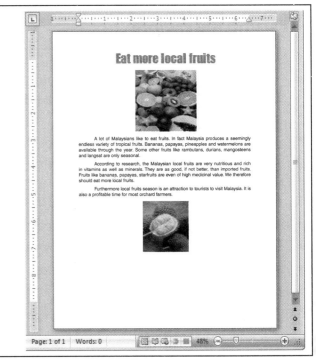

Printing

- Click 🔵 to open Office menu.
- Click 🖨 Print .
- Choose the appropriate printer.
- Ask your teacher for help to set the properties of the printer before you print.
- Click Number of copies: 1 ▲▼ and enter the number of copies to print.
- Make sure the selected printer is switched on and click OK to start printing.

Choose the appropriate printer here.

Creating WordArt design

- The WordArt utility helps us to create impressive banners and labels easily and quickly.
- Open a new blank document.
- Click on Insert tab.
- Click  WordArt ▾. The WordArt Gallery will be displayed. Click on the style as shown by MetalMan below.

Click here.

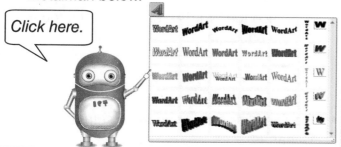

- Type Cambridge ICT Starters.
- Click [OK].

- The WordArt created is as shown below:

Change WordArt

- Click on the WordArt created.
- Click on Format tab.
- Select the style that you like from the WordArt styles and click on it.
- The current style is immediately replaced by the new style selected.
- Click on the new WordArt created.
- Click ▦ Text Wrapping ▾ and select ▦ Square as the text wrapping style.
- Click 📋 to make a copy.
- Click 📋 to make duplicates. The images are now overlapping.
- Move the mouse pointer to the image pasted.

- When the shape of the pointer changes to ✛, hold down the mouse and drag the image to a new position.
- Click on Format tab and change the style to a new style.
- Save your work as WordArt.

Resize WordArt

- You can resize the WordArt created by using a method similar to which you used to resize pictures in the previous section.
- Select any pattern and use ↘, ↗, ↕,or ↔ to drag and resize the WordArt.

- WordArt provides an easy way to create attractive patterns.
- Use WordArt to create the following quotation or any quotation of your own choice.

'Quality is an Art not an Act!'

1.9 Refine and organise

Campaign

- Let us make the text about fruit that you have typed into a campaign poster.
- The objective of the poster is to campaign for people to eat more local fruits.
- You need to refine and reorganise the text and pictures so that they can attract the attention of the target audience, say, your classmates.
- Let us start with the title.

- Use WordArt to create a more appealing title:
  - Open the file fruits5.
  - Delete the title.
  - Click **WordArt** and click to choose a style from the WordArt Gallery.
  - Type the title Eat more local fruits.
  - Adjust the WordArt to a suitable size.
  - Place the WordArt created at the top of the passage.

Italic *I*

- The names of the fruits are mostly local names and some are not common to other countries.
- To stress and to show the audience that they are local names, we can use the italic character style.

- Double-click quickly on the first fruit, Bananas.
- Click *I* to change the style to italic.
- Change the character style of all the names of the fruits to *italic*.
- Save the file as fruits6.

Bold **B** and Underline U

- To further enhance the text, you can make it **bold** and <u>underlined</u>.
- Double-click quickly on the word medicinal.
- Click **B**, U to make it bold and underlined.
- Double-click quickly on the word value.
- Click **B**, U to make it bold and underlined.
- Click 💾 to save the file.

Clicking **B** *once will set the format to* **BOLD**. *Clicking on it again will cancel this format.* U *and* *I* *have the same features.*

Font colours

- To highlight the important message carried by the words nutritious, vitamins and minerals, select the words and change their colours to red.
- Change the colour of all the fruits' names to violet or any other colours that you like.

- Click 💾 to save the changes.

Always save your work after making changes.

Text wrapping style

- The campaign poster will be more eyecatching if we enlarge the picture and use it as background.
- To do this we need to change the layout of the picture.
- Click to select the picture.
- Click ![Text Wrapping] on the Format tab.
- Select ![Behind Text] because we are going to put this picture as background behind the texts.
- If you put the mouse pointer on top of the picture, the pointer will change from I to ⊕.
- This means that you can now move the picture anywhere you like on the page.
- Now click and hold down the mouse, and drag to move the picture to the top left corner.
- Place the mouse pointer at the bottom right of the picture; it will change its shape to ⬉.
- Hold down the mouse and drag diagonally to the right until the complete width of the page is covered.
- Next, place the mouse pointer at the bottom middle of the picture. Its shape is then changed to ⬍.
- Hold down the mouse and drag down until the complete length of the page is covered.
- If you cannot see the text, click ![Text Wrapping] and select ![Behind Text] again.
- To make the text legible, click on the picture. Click on Format tab. In the Adjust group, click ![Brightness] and then ![Picture Corrections Options...] .
- In the dialogue box, type 70% for brightness and --70% for contrast.
- Click ![save icon] to save all the changes.

Move to picture to the top left corner

Drag diagonally to the right to cover the width of the page

Drag down to cover the length of the page

Make the background image pale.

Touching up

- Increase the font size to 18 so that the text covers more of the page. It is also easier to read from a distance.
- We can add more mouth-watering pictures so that the whole poster is more attractive and appealing to our audience.
- Insert the picture langsat.jpg.
- Change the text wrapping style to square.
- Resize to a suitable size and move it to the top right corner of the first paragraph.
- Insert another picture, rambutan.jpg.
- Change the text wrapping style to square.
- Resize to a suitable size and move it to the left of the second paragraph.
- Select the picture durian.jpg.
- Change the text wrapping style to square.
- Resize to a suitable size and move it to the right of the last paragraph.
- Add another WordArt at the bottom, otherwise the poster is not balanced!
- Click and choose a style.
- Type Nutritious & Delicious!
- Save your final poster as CPoster.

A lot of Malaysians like to eat imported fruits. In fact Malaysia produces a seemingly endless variety of tropical fruits. *Bananas, papayas, pineapples* and *watermelons* are available through the year. Some other fruits like *rambutans, durians, mangosteens* and *langsat* are only seasonal.

According to research, the Malaysian local fruits are very nutritious and rich in vitamins as well as minerals. They are as good, if not better, than imported fruits. Fruits like *bananas, papayas, starfruits* are even of high **medicinal value**. We therefore should eat more local fruits.

Furthermore local fruits season is an attraction to tourists to visit Malaysia. It is also a profitable time for most orchard farmers.

Nutritious & Delicious!

Adding a page border

- As a finishing touch, let us add a page border so that the poster is even more eye catching to your classmates.
- On the Page Layout tab, click ☐ Page Borders in the Page Background group.
- Click ▾ at Art: to see a drop-down list of borders.
- Scroll down until you find the border that you like.
- Click on it to select.
- Look at the Preview panel. Choose another art if you do not like the one chosen.
- Click OK to insert the page border selected.
- Click 🖫 to save the final copy.
- Print a copy of your work and paste it on the next page.

Click here to see a list of borders. Click on the one you like.

Evaluation of the finished poster

- Now let us evaluate the poster that we have created.
- We used WordArt to create the title to make it more impressive and eye-catching.
- We used different font styles, *italic*, **bold** and <u>underlined</u>, to stress and enhance important text.
- We used colour to highlight the important messages carried by some of the words.
- We used font colour to make the names of the local fruits stand out.
- We added appropriate photos to attract the audience's attention even before they read the text in detail.
- We made the background art pale so the text can be read easily.
- Finally we added a page border to further enhance the beauty and attractiveness of the poster.

Print a copy and glue your printed copy on this page.

It is all right to cover me!

Sample copy of work done

Open Day

- Your school Parents-Teachers Association is organising an Open Day.
- You are required to help to type the following brochure (do not make any changes):

SIMPLY FUN-TASTIC

SPPS Parent-Teacher Ass. proudly presents:

St Peter Pri. School's Open Day
Date   :   15 August
Time   :   11 a.m. to 6 p.m.
Place   :   St. Peter's Kindergarten

- Save the brochure as OpenDay.
- Complete the brochure by copying all the text from the file WhatWeHave.docx.
- Save your file again.

Editing

- After reading through the draft that you have typed, the PTA have requested that you make the following adjustments:
- Make the following changes to the title so that it has:
  - a size of 16 point
  - a Times New Roman font
  - an <u>underline</u> and *italic* font style
  - centre alignment.
- Make the following changes to the body text of the brochure so that it has:
  - a size of 12 point
  - a `Courier New` font
  - centre alignment.

> *I must remember the date and time of the Open Day!*

- Type out the complete words:
  - type the word Ass. in full: Association
  - type the word Pri. in full: Primary.
- Correct the date and time and make them **bold**:
  - the date of the Open Day has been changed to 4 July
  - the place has also been changed to St Peter's Primary School.

More editing

- Insert the words for you before the colon at the end of the sentence What we have in store:.
- There will not be any Mathematics Quiz. Delete Mathematics.
- Replace Drawing competition with Colouring competition.
- The Tug O'War between parents and children should be Tug O'War between parents and teachers.
- Next, use cut and paste to rearrange the activities into the following order:
  1. Colouring competition   (4-6 years old)
  2. Science Quiz   (7-9 years old)
  3. Talent Time   (10-12 years old)
  4. Tug O'War between parents and teachers
  5. Food stalls selling mouth-watering food at reasonable prices
- Save your edited text as a new file, OpenDay2.

Insert graphics

Insert a page border of balloons.

Insert another graphic (partytime.jpg or any relevant graphic) at the end of the document.

Refining the brochure

- The PTA is very pleased with your work.
- They have decided to make it into a brochure and distribute it to all the children in the school.
- You are now required to refine the way the text and image appear on the page to make your brochure more appealing and appropriate for its audience (your schoolmates). To complete this task, you may:
  - change the font style, size and colour;
  - replace the image or add new images of your own choice;
  - **or** work on the whole document and reorganise the contents and/or change the formatting based on your own choices so that it suits your audience better.
- Save your completed work as brochure.

Self-evaluation

- Use the space provided below to explain how the changes you have made improve the document and make it more appealing to your audience.

_____

_____

_____

_____

Optional extension and challenge activities

Module 1 – Exploring Documents

Challenge 1

- Use Word Art and clip art pictures or shapes to make a greetings card for a friend.

Challenge 2

- List some of the rules for a favourite game.
- Save the list.
- Open the list and turn it into a poster with headings and images to make it attractive so people will want to read it.

Optional extension and challenge activities

Challenge 3

- Make a poster to tell people to eat healthy food and exercise daily.
- Remember to centre some of the headings and to use colour and different sized fonts to make the poster attractive.
- Give it a border and a coloured background.

Module 2
Exploring Images

Learning Objectives

	Student is able to:	Pass/Merit
1	Create repeating patterns using stamps and/or copy tools	P
2	Create pictures using a variety of tools and effects	P
3	Select appropriate objects, copy and resize them	M
4	Save drafts showing the development of the design	M

2.1 Paint

Starting Paint

- Launch Paint.
- Is the white drawing area a full screen size?
- If not, place the mouse pointer at the bottom right corner of the white drawing area.
- When it changes its shape to ⤡, drag down diagonally until you get a full screen size.
- Hover the pointer over any of the document handles and drag to alter the size or shape of the drawing area.

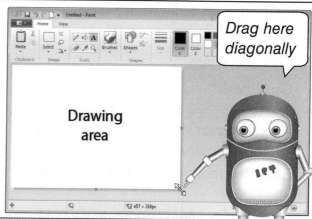

Drag here diagonally

Drawing area

Import image

- Click .
- Click 📋 Paste from.
- Select the file balloons.jpg and click Open.
- The image is placed at the top left corner.

You can import more than 1 image using 📋 Paste from, but you can only import 1 image at a time using Open.

The imported graphic.

2.2 Creating patterns

Duplicate images

- Click [Copy].

- Click [Paste] again.

- Click Paste.

- You will not see the pasted image because it is pasted on top of the original image in the top left corner.

- Place the mouse pointer on top of the image.

- When the pointer changes to ✛ hold down the mouse and drag to the right so that the two images are side by side.

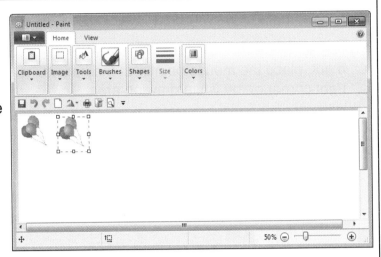

Repeated patterns

- Click [Select].

- Drag around the two images.

- Use the **copy and paste** method to duplicate the two images.

- Move the pasted image to the right. You should now get 4 images arranged in a row.

- Repeat the **copy and paste** process and arrange the images in a row at the top to form the top border.

- You can copy and paste 1, 2, 4 and then 8 images to speed up the process.

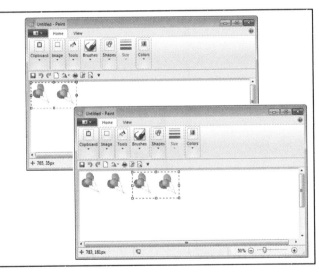

Border

- Copy the whole row at the top.
- Paste the image and drag it to the bottom to form the bottom border.
- Can you complete the border on both sides?
- Save your design as border1.
- Create new border designs using the graphics bird.jpg and cup.jpg.
- Save your designs as border2 and border3.

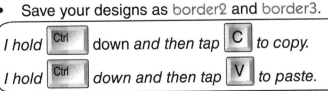

I hold [Ctrl] *down and then tap* [C] *to copy.*

I hold [Ctrl] *down and then tap* [V] *to paste.*

Design 1

- Click 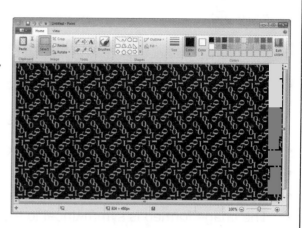.
- Click Paste from.
- Select pattern1.jpg or any other of the patterns given.
- Use the copy and paste method to duplicate the imported graphic.
- This time, instead of arranging them into a border, arrange them very close together to form a continuous design.
- Repeat the **copy and paste** process until the whole work space is filled with the graphic.
- Save it as design1.

Design 2

- Repeat the previous exercise using the graphic pattern2.jpg.
- Save the work as design2.

From a simple design to a repeated pattern – it is marvellous!

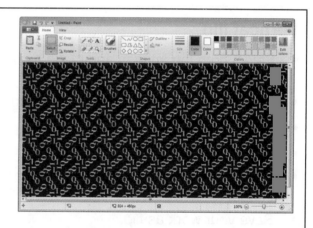

Resize imported graphic

- Import the graphics bird.jpg.
- Place the cursor at the bottom right corner of the image.
- When the cursor changes its shape to ↖, hold down the mouse button and drag towards the image to reduce its size.
- Save it as bird2.

Drag towards the image to reduce it or drag away from the image to enlarge it.

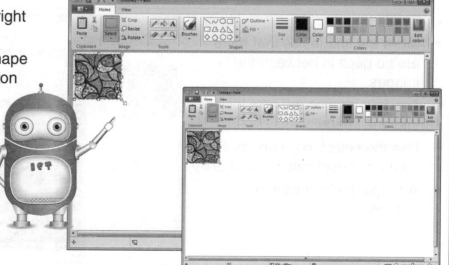

2.3 Symmetry

Symmetry

- Click 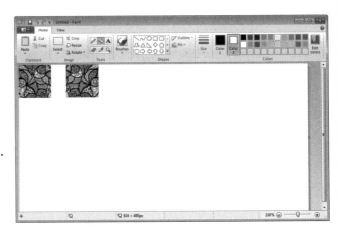 Paste.
- Click ⊞ Paste from and open the file you have saved in the previous exercise, bird2.
- Select and copy the image and place the images side by side.
- Use selection tool Select to select the second image.
- Click ⟲ Rotate ▾.
- Select option ◢◣ Flip horizontal.
- The image formed is symmetrical to the original image.
- Save your work as symmetry.

Vertical flip

- Select both the images and make a copy of them.
- Place it exactly below the original images.
- Click ⟲ Rotate ▾.
- Select option ◥ Flip vertical.
- You have just produced another symmetrical image.
- Save your work as flip.

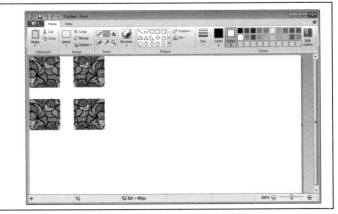

New pattern

- Open the file flip again.
- Move the images so that there are no gaps in between the images.
- The four images are now joined into one image.
- Use the select, copy and paste method to duplicate the image.
- Arrange the images into a pattern.

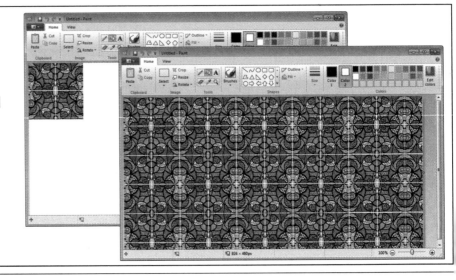

2.4 Designing a card

Birthday card

- The theme of the design is Birthday card.
- Start Paint with a new page.
- Adjust the drawing area to full screen size.
- With ▢ blue fill the background with light blue.
- Import the image balloons.jpg.
- Copy the image and paste it beside the first.
- Give it a horizontal flip.
- Repeat the pattern to form the top border.
- Copy the top border and place it as the bottom border.
- Give the bottom border a vertical flip.

- Use copy and paste, flip vertically or horizontally to complete the vertical borders on both sides.
- Save the picture as birthdaycard1.

Birthday cake

- Import another image, birthdaycake.jpg.
- Place it at the bottom centre of the picture.
- Save your picture as birthdaycard2.
- Adjust the cake's size so that it is about half the height of the picture.
- Save your picture again as birthdaycard3.
- It is useful to save your picture regularly with a new filename each time so that you have a series of files to show the progress of creating the picture.

Present

- Follow the steps below to draw a present box.

  1. Make ▪ Black and ▢ White.
  2. Click rectangle tool ▢ and solid colour and draw a box shape.
  3. Use the Line tool ◺ to draw a right-angle slightly above and to the right of the rectangle, as in the diagram.
  4. Use the Line tool ◺ to join the corners to form a box. Remember! Leave no gaps!

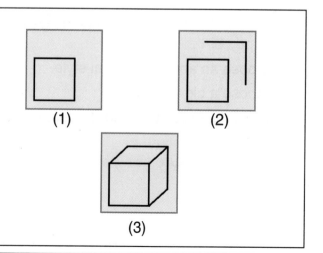

(1)   (2)   (3)

Putting on ribbons

- Use to fill the 3 visible sides of the present box with appropriate colours.
- Select red colour and the thickest line width.
- Draw the ribbons.
- Use **Brushes** tool with the brush shape to draw a knot on top of the ribbon.

Duplicate the present

- Copy and paste the image of the present box.
- Move the pasted image to an appropriate position above the original present box.
- Reduce its size slightly.
- Paste another image of the original present box to the right side of the cake.
- Give it a horizontal flip. Fill the sides with different colours.
- Make a duplicate of this image.
- Place the new duplicated new image above the third present box.

- Reduce its size slightly.
- Save this picture as birthdaycard4.

Adding greeting words

- Use the Text tool **A** to write the greeting 'Happy Birthday'.
- Choose an appropriate font style.
- Choose a big font size.
- Adjust the greeting at the top centre of the card.
- Save your picture as birthdaycard5.

Poster

- Create a poster with the theme Clearance Sale.
- Before you start, you must try to think of the final layout of your picture so that you can work towards completing the picture to that layout.

- You can either use your own scanned images or images from other suitable sources, or have your teacher provide the images.
- It is important that you save your work in stages to show the development of the poster.

Stage 1

- Start with a blank full-screen drawing area.
- Create repeating patterns.
- Import an image, e.g. flower.jpg.
- Place it about 4 to 5 cm from the top border.
- Save your work as poster version1a.
- Use the copy and paste method to create a repeated pattern. You can include symmetry.
- Fill the area above the repeated pattern created with green or any other colour of your choice.
- Type a big title Clearance Sale on top.

- Save your work as poster version1b.

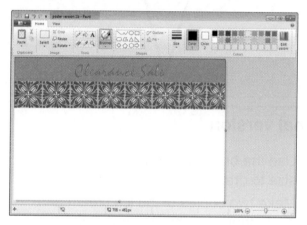

Stage 2

- Use 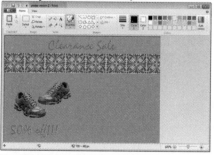 to import the image shoe.jpg.
- Make a duplicate of it and give the image a horizontal flip.
- Adjust the images so that they form a pair of shoes. Place the pair of shoes at the left side of the empty space below the title.
- Fill the rest of the white space with green or any colour of your choice.
- Type a big label 50% off!!!.
- Save your work as poster version 2.

- Follow the next few steps to draw the free gift, ice cream.
  - Draw a small circle with a thick outline.

  - Erase about 10% of the bottom part.

  - Use the brush tool to draw a wavy line across.

Creating an image

- Use the line tool to draw two straight lines to complete the drawing of the ice cream. Be sure to leave no gaps!

- Use the Airbrush tool to fill the ice cream part.
- Fill the cup with suitable colours.

Final version

- Use the brush tool with a suitable brush size to draw some lines on the cup.
- Make two copies of the ice cream and paste them side by side with the original ice cream.
- Change the colour of the ice cream to violet and pink.
- Use the text tool and a big font to put a label above the ice creams. Use:
  Free ice cream for any purchase above $50!
- Save your final version as poster final version.

Optional extension and challenge activities

Module 2 – Exploring Images

Challenge 1

- Create a repeating pattern.
- Use it to make a border for a bookmark.
- Add text to show who owns the bookmark.

Challenge 2

- Use the Line tool to create a horizon on the screen.
- Use the spray and flood fill tools to colour the sky and the land.
- Use the brush, pen and shape tools to add trees or buildings in the foreground.

Challenge 3

- Use the drawing and text tools to make an advertisement for a new type of sweet.

Module 3
Exploring Spreadsheets

Learning Objectives

	Student is able to:	Pass/Merit
1	Enter labels and numbers into a spreadsheet	P
2	Enter and copy simple formulas	P
3	Create a graph	P
4	Modify data	M
5	Use a spreadsheet to answer a modelled scenario ('what if...?')	M

3.1 What is a spreadsheet?

Cells

- Load 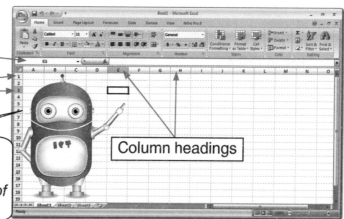 Microsoft Office Excel 2007 .
- A blank spreadsheet is displayed.

Cell address

Row headings

Spreadsheets are made up of cells. Each cell has an address. The address of this cell is E3.

Column headings

Patterns

- Put an X in each of these cells:
  - A2, A3, A4, A5
  - B2, C2, D2, E2, F2
  - B5, C5, D5, E5, F5
  - F3, F4

What pattern have you made?

_____

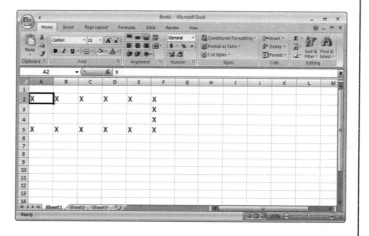

Columns and rows

- Drag along a row.
- Drag down a column.

This is a column.

This is a row.

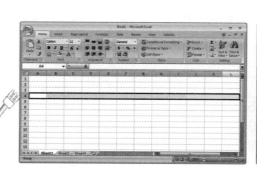

3.2 Autosum Σ

Autosum

- Type a list of five numbers in column A.

- Tap ⬅Enter after typing each number to go to the next cell below.

- Click in cell A6.

- Double-click the autosum icon Σ.

- This will insert a simple formula
  =SUM(A1:A5) for finding the sum of the numbers from A1 to A5.

You can see the formula here.

This adds the numbers in the column.

Animal types

- Look at the animals in this set.
- Count the rabbits, cats and birds.
- Complete the following table:

Animals	
Cats	
Rabbits	
Birds	
Total	

- Type the data in a spreadsheet with the names of the animals in column A, starting from cell A1 as shown in the spreadsheet on the right.

- Type in the number of each type of animal in column B.

- Click in cell B4.

- Double-click the autosum icon Σ.

- What is the total number of animals?

- The total number of animals is

_____

More additions

- Type in the numbers in columns C, D, E and F as shown in the spreadsheet on the right.

- Use autosum Σ to calculate the totals for columns C, D, E and F.

- Write your answers below:

Animals				
Cats	4	8	9	45
Rabbits	7	3	12	23
Birds	9	5	23	78
Total				

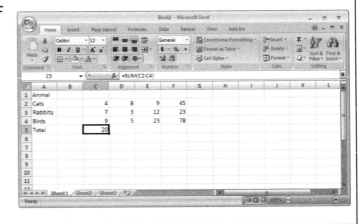

Football scores

- The table on the right shows a list of football players in one column.
- The other column shows how many goals they have scored.
- You can replace the names with those of the players in your favourite team.
- Open a new spreadsheet and key in the names of the players in column A and their scores in column B.

Players	Score
Paulo Di Cario	9
Joe Cole	2
Frank Lampard	2
Frederic Kanoute	8
Trevor Sinclair	3
Total	

Autofit

- Do you notice that when you type the numbers of goals in column B, the names in column A are partly covered?
- This is because the default width of the first column is not wide enough.
- Place the mouse pointer in between the column heads of column A and column B until it changes its shape to ✛.
- Double-click the left mouse button and the column width will be adjusted automatically to fit the longest name.
- You can also drag the mouse pointer ✛ to the right or left to adjust the width manually.

Double-click here to adjust the width of column A according to the longest name.

Total goals

- Click to activate cell B6.
- Double-click the autosum icon **Σ** to get the total of goals scored.
- You can also type the formula manually: =SUM(B1:B5).
- Increase the number scored by Joe Cole to 5.
- Without doing anything, the total has already increased automatically.
- Reduce the number scored by Frederic Kanoute to 6.
- Has the total decreased automatically?

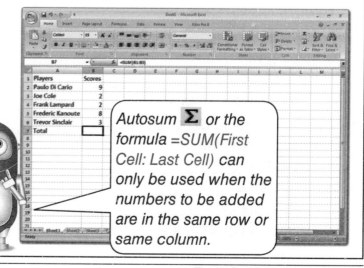

*Autosum **Σ** or the formula =SUM(First Cell: Last Cell) can only be used when the numbers to be added are in the same row or same column.*

3.4 Typing formulas

An adding machine

- Type 3 in cell A1 and 4 in B1.
- Click on C1 and type =.
- Click on A1.
- Tap $\boxed{+}$ on the number pad (or hold $\boxed{\text{Shift}}$ down and then tap $\boxed{+ \atop =}$).
- Click on B1.
- Click ✔ (or tap $\boxed{\leftarrow \text{Enter}}$).
- Cell C1 shows the sum of A1 and B1.
- Change the number in A1 to 5 and tap $\boxed{\leftarrow \text{Enter}}$; the sum in C1 will change automatically to 9.

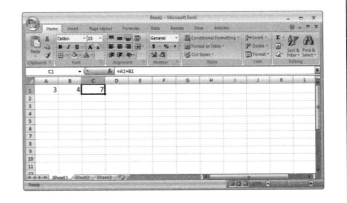

Typing the formula

- Type 6 in cell A2 and 8 in cell B2.
- At C2, instead of using the mouse pointer, you can type the cell addresses directly: =A2+B2.
- Tap $\boxed{\leftarrow \text{Enter}}$ to see the sum.
- At D2, type =A1+B1+A2+B2 and tap $\boxed{\leftarrow \text{Enter}}$.
- D2 is the sum of all the four numbers in A1, B1, A2, and B2.

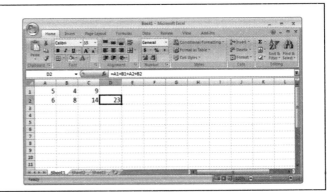

Exercise

- Write down the answers in the spaces provided.
- Use the SUM function to find out the answer for the following additions:
  - 17 + 18 = _____
  - 23 + 55 = _____
  - 434 + 259 = _____
  - 4699 + 8977 + 233 = _____

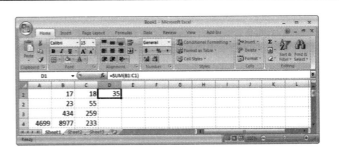

- Use the simple addition formula to answer the following additions:
  - 31 + 33 = _____
  - 126 + 43 = _____
  - 467 + 344 = _____
  - 2355 + 3412 + 7788 = _____

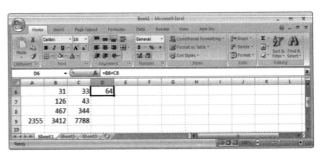

3.5 More formulas

Learning Objective: 2

A subtraction machine

- Click [ ] to start a new worksheet.
- Type 8 in A1 and 1 in B1.
- Click on C1 and type =.
- Click on A1 and tap [−].
- Click on B1.
- Click ✔ (or tap [←Enter]).
- Cell C1 shows A1 subtract B1.
- The formula used was =A1− B1.
- Change the number in A1 to 10, tap [←Enter] and the value in C1 will change to 9 automatically.

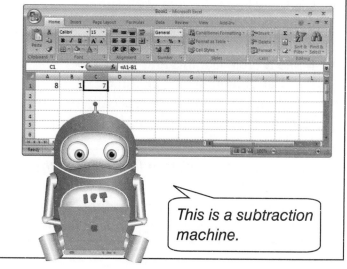

This is a subtraction machine.

Exercise

- Use the simple subtraction formula to answer the following subtractions:
  - 23 − 5 = _____
  - 433 − 29 = _____
  - 5897 − 3328 = _____
  - 4566 − 987 = _____
  - 10045 − 9854 = _____
  - 110107 − 3786 = _____

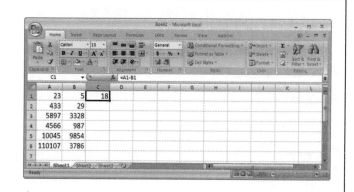

A multiplication machine

- Click [ ] to start a new worksheet.
- Type 3 in A1, 4 in B1.
- Click on C1 and type =.
- Click on A1, Tap [*] or hold [Shift] and tap [*8].
- Click on B1.
- Click ✔ (Or tap [←Enter].)
- C1 will give the product of 3 and 4 with the formula = A1 * B1.
- Change the value in A1 to 5 and tap [←Enter], C1 will become 20 automatically.

*The computer uses * to represent multiplication. When you multiply numbers, the answer is the product.*

How many legs?

- Click ☐ to start a new worksheet.
- Look back at the picture of cats, dogs and birds on page 32.
- Make a table like this and enter the number of animals in column C.
- In column D, type the multiplication formula to work out how many legs in total for each animal.

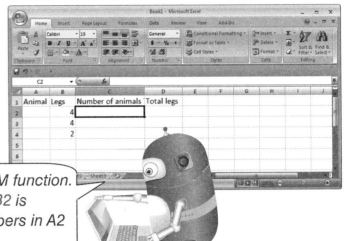

> It is a common mistake to use * with the SUM function. =SUM(A2*B2) is **not** a correct formula. A2*B2 is sufficient for finding the **product** of the numbers in A2 and B2. SUM is used for finding **totals** only.

A division machine

- Click ☐ to start a new worksheet.
- Type 24 in A1 and 3 in B1.
- Click on C1 and type =.
- Click on A1.
- Tap / .
- Click on B1.
- Click ✔ (or tap ⏎ Enter).
- Cell C1 shows the value of A1 divided by B1.
- The computer uses / instead of ÷ for division.

> / is called the forward slash or slash key. Do not confuse it with the backslash key \ .

Giving out sweets

- You have 120 sweets you want to give to 5 friends.
- Set out a spreadsheet like this.
- How many sweets can each of your friends have?
- Oh no! You have forgotten about your best friend Siti! The sweets should be divided by 6 instead of 5.
- How many sweets can each of your friends have now?
- If you have 847 sweets and 7 friends, use column C to find out how many sweets you need to give to each of your 7 friends.

> You will need to use a dividing formula.

Survey

Ask your friends how many of these things they would like to spend money on each week.

Comics
sweets
CDs
cinema
fares
magazines

- Enter the information on a spreadsheet to see how much pocket money your friends need.

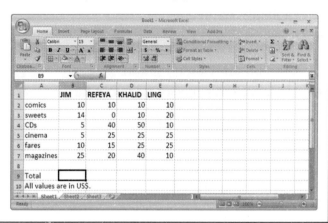

Copying and pasting formulas

- In cell B9, use Σ to find the total money needed.
- You can easily copy the formula to other cells without re-typing it.
- The cell references will change automatically when the formula is placed in a different cell:
  - Click on cell B9.
  - Click 📄.
  - Click on C9 and click 📋.
  - Click on D9 and click 📋.
  - Click on E9 and click 📋.

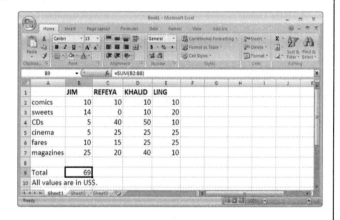

Copying by drag and drop

- You can also copy formulas by **drag and drop**.
- Click on the cell with the formula that you want to copy.
- Place the mouse pointer at the bottom right corner so that its shape changes to **+**.
- Hold down the left mouse button and drag to the cells into which you want to copy and paste the formula.
- Release the mouse button.

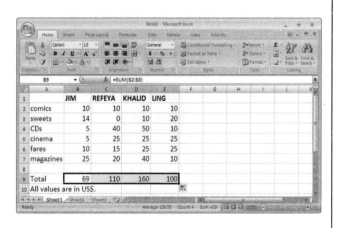

3.7 Drawing graphs

Column graph

- Draw a graph showing what Jim spends his pocket money on.
- Highlight A2 to B7.
- Click on Insert tab.
- Choose the column graph .
- In Chart Tools, click on Layout tab, then click 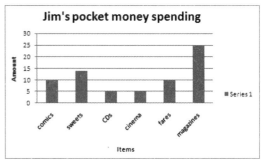, and.
- Write a suitable title for the graph. The title should be related to the data that you want to display.

Completing the graph

- Give the x-axis and y-axis a suitable label each.
- We can still make adjustments to the graph, like changing the font size and font style.
- Enlarge the graph horizontally so that the labels of the items are aligned horizontally.
- Make sure that the labels for all 6 items are shown clearly.
- Click on the title. Change its colour to red, font size to 14 and font style to Underlined.
- As we do not need the legend which only shows the meaningless 'Series 1', click on it to select and then tap Delete to remove it.
- Save your worksheet as expenditure.

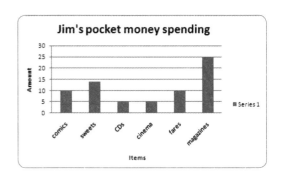

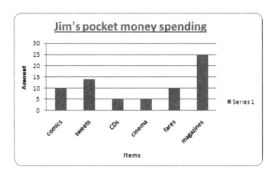

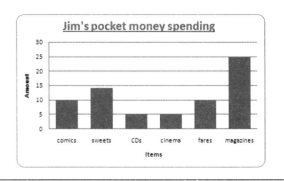

Pie chart

- Instead of a column or bar chart, you can also use a pie chart to display the information.
- Go back to sheet 1 and highlight the same data, A2 to B7.
- Click on Insert tab.
- Click [Pie] for Chart type.
- Select 3-D Pie for chart sub-type.

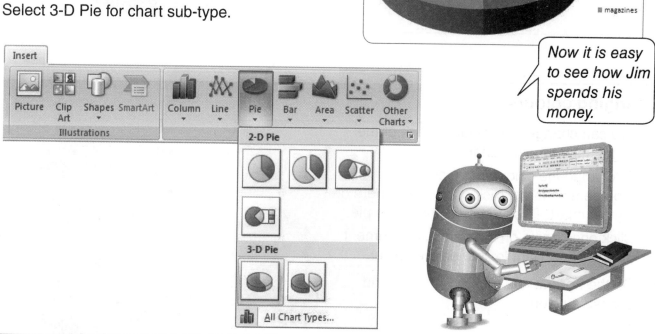

Now it is easy to see how Jim spends his money.

Data labels

- Click the pie chart to open the Design tab and click on the Chart Layouts group.
- Click on each chart in turn to see the effect.
- Click to show the percentage.

Click here to see the percentages.

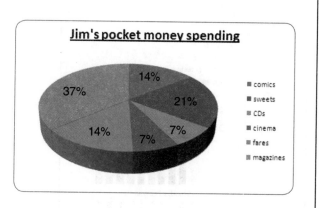

Interpreting the graph

- Without referring back to the table of data, based on the pie chart created, Jim spent the largest portion of his pocket money on which of the items?

_____

- What can you say about the amount he spent on fares and comics?

_____

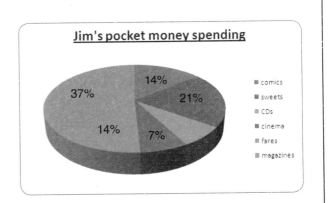

Changing colours

- You can change the colour of each of the segments of the pie chart.
- To change the colour of the segment representing fares, click once somewhere on the pie chart. This will select the entire pie.
- Click once again on the particular segment of which you want to change the colour.
- On the Format tab, click [Shape Fill ▼] and choose a colour.

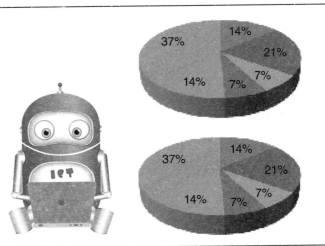

Colour scheme

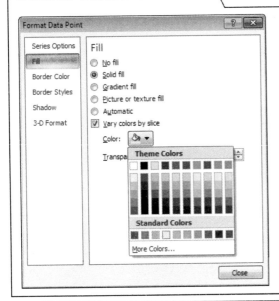

- Choose new colours for each segment.
- Pick the desired colour and click [OK].
- Save your work again.

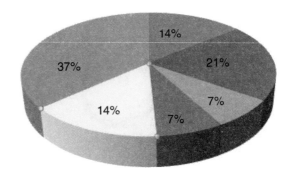

More graphs

- Draw a column chart to show Khalid's weekly expenditure.
- First highlight the items comics, sweets, etc.
- Hold down [Ctrl] and highlight the data for Khalid.
- Click on Insert tab and choose a 3-D column graph.
- Click [Move Chart] in the Location group and choose new sheet and call it Khalid.
- Write a suitable Chart title and label the x- and y-axes accordingly.
- Click Legend and select [None Turn off Legend].
- Click on series 1 label and delete.
- Click on Design tab, click on move chart and place the chart 'As new sheet:' Khalid.
- Save your worksheet using the same file name.
- Print a copy of this graph and glue it in the space below.
- Draw similar charts for Refeya and Ling.

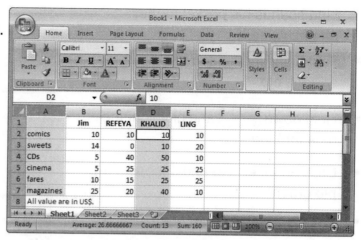

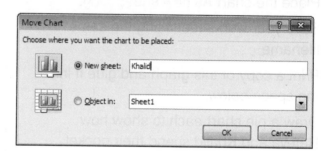

Do you know why the graph for Refeya does not show any column for sweets?

Glue your column chart here. It is all right for you to cover me.

3.8 More graphs

Another pie chart

- Draw a pie chart to show what Ling spends his pocket money on each week.

- First highlight the items comics, sweets, etc.

- Hold down Ctrl and highlight the data for Ling.

- Click on Insert tab and choose a 3-D pie graph.

- Write a suitable Chart title.

- Place the chart 'As new sheet:' Ling.

- Save your worksheet using the same filename.

- Print a copy of this graph and glue it in the space below.

- Draw a pie chart each to show how Refeya and Khalid spend their pocket money each week.

- Do you know why the pie chart for Refeya has only 5 segments?

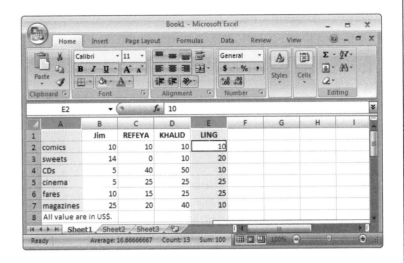

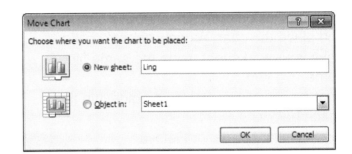

Glue your graph here. It is all right for you to cover me.

3.9 Completing data

Completing data

- The school Science Club wants to raise funds for their annual activities by taking part in the school food fair.
- The club's target is $500.
- Open the MS Excel file budget.
- Complete the list of items.
- Fill in the quantity column in the table based on the quantity given.
- Save the file as budgetl.

Item	Quantity
Cola	96
Lemonade	96
Orange juice	120
Mineral water	50
Burger	50
Fried chicken wing	100
Cake	30
Fried noodle	50
Watermelon	50
Papaya	50

Calculation

- The cost price for Cola is its **unit cost price x quantity**.
- Click on the first cell under Cost Price (E4) and tap =.
- Click on the first cell under Unit Cost Price (D4).
- Tap *.
- Click on the first cell under Quantity (C4).
- Click ✓ or tap [←Enter].
- Copy the formula from E4 to the rest of the cells under Cost Price.

> You can type the formula =D4*C4 directly in cell E4.

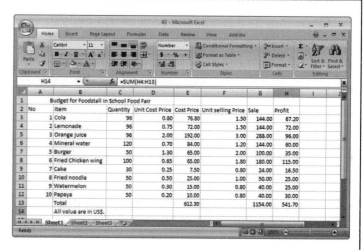

- The sale for Cola is its **unit selling price x quantity**.
- Click on the first cell under Sale (G4) and tap =.
- Click on the first cell under Unit Selling Price (F4) and tap *.
- Click on the first cell under Quantity (C4).
- You can also type the formula =F4*C4 directly in cell G4.
- Click ✓ or tap [←Enter].
- Copy the formula from G4 to the rest of the cells under Sale.
- Save your worksheet again.

Target

- Profit for selling Cola is the difference between the cost price and the sale (H4=G4−E4).
- Click on H4 and tap =.
- Click on G4 and tap − (the minus sign).
- Click on E4.
- Click ✓ or tap [←Enter].
- Copy the formula to the rest of the cells under Profit.
- Use the SUM function to find the **total cost price**, **total sale** and **total profit**.
- Can the club achieve its target?
- Save the worksheet using the same file name.

3.10 What if...?

Change data

- It was found that the unit cost prices for some of the items were wrongly quoted.
- The correct unit cost prices are as follow:
  - Burger – $1.50
  - Fried chicken wing – $0.85
- With these changes in price, do you think the club can still achieve the target of $500?
- Adjust the unit cost prices as above.
- Save your adjusted spreadsheet as budget2.
- Was your prediction correct? _____

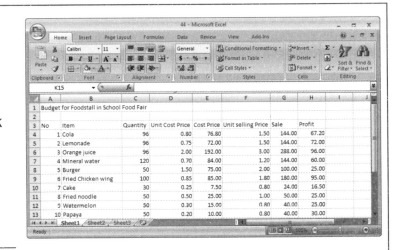

Actual sale

- During the actual fair, what if some of the items were not completely sold?
- Do you think the club can still reach the target of $500? _____
- Insert a column in between columns E and F: select column F. Click [Insert ▾] on the Home Tab then select [Insert Cells].
- Enter the column head as Quantity Sold.
- Enter the quantities sold in this new column F.
- You will need to change the formula for Sale.
- The formula for Sale for Cola is now **quantity sold x unit selling price**.
- Copy this formula to the rest of the cells in column H.
- Use the SUM function to find the **total actual sale**.
- Was your prediction correct? _____
- Draw a column chart to show the profit for each item.
- Place the chart below the spreadsheet.
- Save your work as budget3.
- Based on the graph, which item has the highest profit?

  _____

Item	Quantity Sold
Cola	96
Lemonade	88
Orange juice	80
Mineral water	111
Burger	50
Fried chicken wing	98
Cake	25
Fried noodle	48
Watermelon	44
Papaya	45

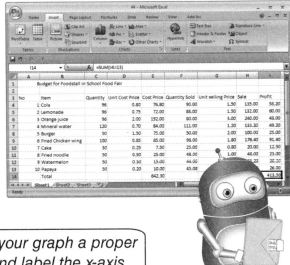

Give your graph a proper title and label the x-axis and y-axis accordingly.

3.11 Evidence

Formula

- Open budget3 if you have closed it.

- You can show all the formulas that you have used in this worksheet as evidence that you have done the worksheet correctly.

- Click on Formulas tab.

- Click **Show Formulas**.

- Note that instead of the calculated values, the formulas are now displayed.

- Click the **Show Formulas** again to hide them.

- As some of the formula are longer than the default column width, you need to adjust the column width.

- Save this version of your worksheet as budget4.

Printing

- Print a copy of budget4, showing all the formulas used.
- Glue the printed page on this page.

Glue your printed copies here. I don't mind if you cover me!

More printing

- Print budget3, showing the worksheet and the graph.
- Glue the printout on this page as evidence of your hard work.

Optional extension and challenge activities

Module 3 – Exploring Spreadsheets

Challenge 1

- Make a table to show how many people in your class wear glasses and how many do not.
- Design a spreadsheet to show this information.
- Use it to draw a simple bar chart.
- Remember to label the axes and give the chart a title.

Challenge 2

- Find out which are the favourite snack foods for the people in your class.
- Make a pie chart to show your results.
- What can you tell about the types of snacks people prefer by looking at the chart?

Challenge 3

- See what Ali uses to make 15 buns
  2 eggs
  100g sugar
  80g butter
  125g flour
- Use a spreadsheet to find what he will need to make 60 or 120 buns.

Module 4
Exploring Databases

Learning Objectives

	Student is able to:	Pass/Merit
1	Add new records to a data file	P
2	Identify field types	P
3	Use 'equals', 'more than' and 'less than' in searches	P
4	Re-phrase a given question in terms of search criteria	M
5	Interpret data	M

4.1 Exploring databases

What words mean

- **Data** is information.
  - The ages of your friends are data.
  - What food you like best is data.
- A **database** is a collection of data. Your list of birthdays for friends is a database. Your teacher's class register is a database. You can use Microsoft Access to make a database.
- **Fields** are the headings under which you put data. You might want to collect data about pets. The number of legs might be one field. Their weight might be another field.

- A **record** is a set of data about one particular thing or person. In a database about people in your class, each record would be given the name of a person in the class. In a database about dinosaurs, each record would be given the name of a dinosaur.
- A **file** is a collection of records. All the records of people in your class might be called 'Class 5A'. All your dinosaur records might be called 'Dinosaurs'. The file name is the name you use to save your computer database.

Test yourself

- Check that you understand the words by filling in these blanks.

  Jim Kelly had some d _ _ a on ways to travel. He wrote his dat _ _ _ _ e on paper. Then he put it on the computer. He made it into a f _ _ _ called 'Travel'. This f _ _ _ had re _ _ _ _ _ of all the different ways to travel. Each record had a f _ _ _ _ called 'Number of wheels'. It was difficult for Jim to fill that f _ _ _ _ in the jumbo jet re _ _ _ _. When he saved his f _ _ _ in the computer he called it 'JKtravel'.

Microsoft Access 🗝

- Click 🪟 to open Start menu.
- Click ▶ **All Programs** .
- Click 🗝 Microsoft Office Access 2007 .
- Click 📂 open.
- Select the file survey.
- Click | Open |▼| .

Select the file survey.

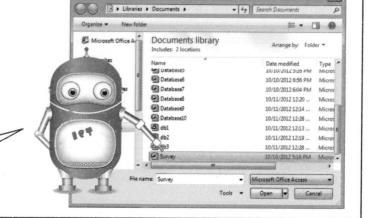

4.2 Database basic

Look through the records

- Click .
- Double-click on **frm_survey** to view an individual record.

Click here to view individual records.

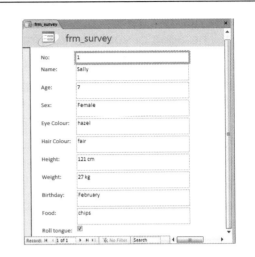

Look at the file

- Look at the bottom of the screen to see the record information.

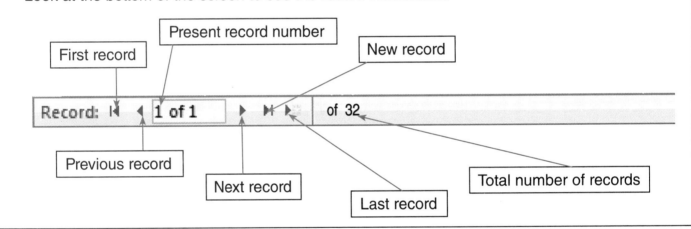

Present record number

First record

New record

Record: ⊮ ⊲ 1 of 1 ▶ ⊮ ⊳ of 32

Previous record

Next record

Last record

Total number of records

Viewing records

- Click ▶ until you get to record number 10.
- What is the name of the child?

- How old is the child?

- Is the child a boy or a girl?

- What is the child's eye colour?

- How tall is the child?

- What is the child's weight?

- In which month was the child born?

- What is the child's favourite food?

- Can the child roll his or her tongue?

Spreadsheet format

- You can view the records in the spreadsheet format.

- Double-click 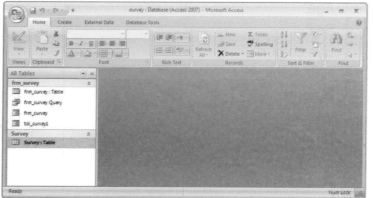 tbl_Survey : Table .

- Use this format to find out if these are True (T) or False (F).

  - Sam is 7 years old.....................☐

  - Julia has brown eyes................☐

  - Nicholas likes fish....................☐

  - Kate is taller than 140 cm..........☐

  - Rose was born during Christmas.☐

  - Christopher has brown hair.........☐

  - Jane cannot roll her tongue.........☐

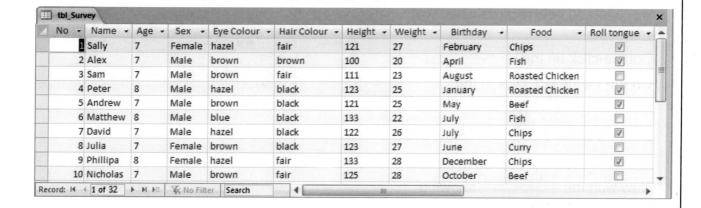

No	Name	Age	Sex	Eye Colour	Hair Colour	Height	Weight	Birthday	Food	Roll tongue
1	Sally	7	Female	hazel	fair	121	27	February	Chips	☑
2	Alex	7	Male	brown	brown	100	20	April	Fish	☑
3	Sam	7	Male	brown	fair	111	23	August	Roasted Chicken	☐
4	Peter	8	Male	hazel	black	123	25	January	Roasted Chicken	☑
5	Andrew	7	Male	brown	black	121	25	May	Beef	☑
6	Matthew	8	Male	blue	black	133	22	July	Fish	☐
7	David	7	Male	hazel	black	122	26	July	Chips	☑
8	Julia	7	Female	brown	black	123	27	June	Curry	☐
9	Phillipa	8	Female	hazel	fair	133	28	December	Chips	☑
10	Nicholas	7	Male	brown	fair	125	28	October	Beef	☐

Record: 1 of 32 | No Filter | Search

Adding new records

- If you are still in the spreadsheet layout format, you will be brought to a new row.

- Select the new row marked with ▶※.

- Ignore the first coloumn for serial number. This number will be inserted automatically by the computer once you have completed the data of a new record.

- Type the new data under the appropriate column headings.

- Do not enter the units for Height and Weight.

Name:	Morris
Age:	8
Sex:	Male
Eye colour:	blue
Hair colour:	fair
Height:	120 (cm)
Weight:	29 (kg)
Birthday:	September
Food:	Chips
Roll tongue:	Yes

More new records

- Add two more records.

- Click ![save icon] to save the newly added records.

Name:	Bernard
Age:	9
Sex:	Male
Eye colour:	blue
Hair colour:	fair
Height:	133 (cm)
Weight:	31(kg)
Birthday:	December
Food:	Ice cream
Roll tongue:	Yes

Name:	Maimunah
Age:	10
Sex:	Female
Eye colour:	black
Hair colour:	black
Height:	125 (cm)
Weight:	28 (kg)
Birthday:	January
Food:	Roasted chicken
Roll tongue:	No

Using form for new records

- You can add new records whenever you need.

- Double-click on the ⬛ frm_survey : Table

- On the Home tab, click in the Views group, click on the downward pointing arrow on View and select the ⬛ Form View. You will now be in Form view with the ⬛ Design View showing so you can toggle back to Design view when needed.

- In the Records group click ⬛ New.

- Add your data to the new record which appears.

- Interview 3 friends and fill in their particulars in the blank forms on this page.

- Use these data to add more records.

- Fill in all the fields on-screen and click ![save icon] to save the newly added records.

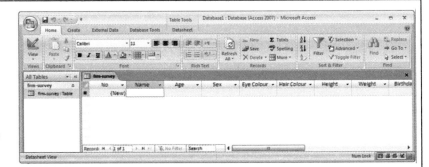

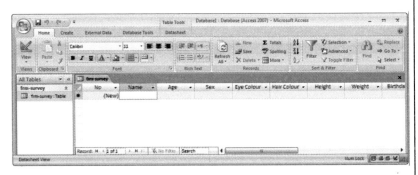

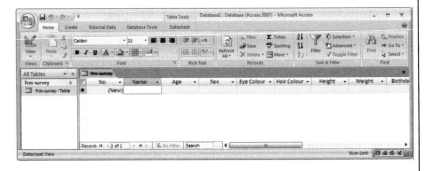

4.4 Evidence of work done

Evidence of adding new records

- After you have added the six records, Double-click 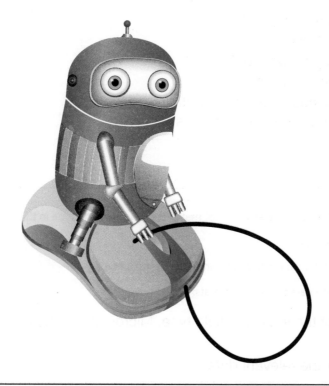 ⊞ tbl_Survey : Table and stay in Datasheet view so that you can see all records.
- Do a snapshot of the six records added. Paste the snapshot in a new MS Word document.
- Save the document as NewRecords.
- Print a copy of NewRecords and glue the hard copy on this page as evidence that you have managed to add six new records.

Glue your printed copy on this page.

Delete record

- Before you delete the record you must select the record to be deleted.
- In Datasheet view, click to select the row with the data you wish to delete.
- Select the record on Morris that you added in the previous exercise.
- Click ✕ Delete.
- A warning message will be displayed.
- Click Yes to confirm.
- Delete one more record: Bernard.

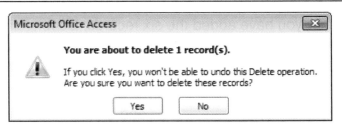

You can highlight more than 1 record and click on ✕ Delete *to delete all the records highlighted.*

Field types

- Every field has a specific field type for a specific purpose.
- AutoNumber: generates numbering automatically.
- Text: most common and used for text-related fields.
- Number: important when calculation is needed.
- Date/Time: date-related field.
- Yes/No: for specific Yes/right or No/wrong answers only.
- Currency: for inputting currency.
- Alphanumeric: mixes numbers' with alphabetic letters (e.g. name and address).

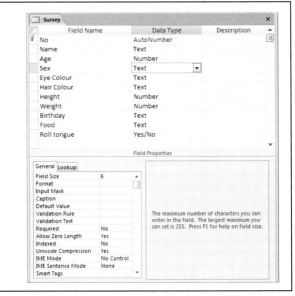

Invalid data

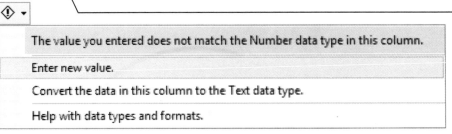

- If you have entered data of the irrelevant field type, Microsoft Access 2007 will prompt a message as shown above.
- Click OK to re-enter the relevant data.

Identify field type

ID	Name	Home town	Pocket money	Number of brothers Sisters	Age	Number of pets	Right handed	Joining date
1	Raymond	Lawas	$20.00	3	16	1	✓	3/3/2012
2	Peter	Ipoh	$50.00	5	21	0	☐	1/6/2011
3	Mary	London	$60.00	2	15	4	☐	3/1/2010
4	Khalid	Malacca	$33.00	12	17	0	✓	6/6/2009
5	Munch	Jakarta	$15.00	6	18	2	✓	9/10/2008
✱	6		$0.00	0	0	0	☐	

- Identify the field type of each of the fields used in the table above:
  - Name – <u>Text</u>_____
  - Home town – _____
  - Pocket money – _____
  - Number of Brothers & Sisters – _____
  - Age – _____
  - Number of pets – _____
  - Right handed – _____
  - Joining date – _____

Finding records

- Click 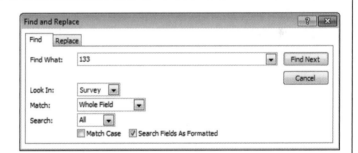 Find.
- To find children that are 133 cm tall, type 133 (without 'cm') in the field Find What: .
- Check that the Look In: field contains the file name Survey.
- Click Find Next .
- The first record meeting your find criteria in Find What: will be displayed.
- Click Find Next to continue to look for records.
- A message will be displayed if there are no more records meeting your criteria.

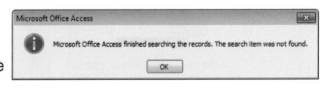

Be accurate

- In the above example, a child with weight 133 kg will also appear as part of the result.
- To be more specific, you can first click on the field that you wish to search through.
- After typing the criteria in Find What: , ensure that the appropriate field name appears in Look In: .
- Click Find Next to start finding the records.
- You must be accurate in writing your criteria in Find What: .

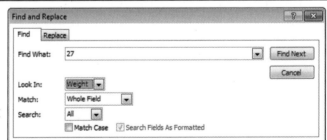

- If you are finding names, ensure that the names that you are typing are correct.
- You will not find Matthew if you type Mathew, missing a 't'.

4.6 Query

Create query

- We use query to find records with conditions.
- Click on Create tab.
- Click  Query Wizard .
- Select **Simple Query Wizard** and click OK .
- A Simple Query Wizard will be displayed.
- Make sure that under Tables/Queries, the table selected is tbl_Survey.
- Click **>>** to select all the fields.
- Click **Next >** to continue.

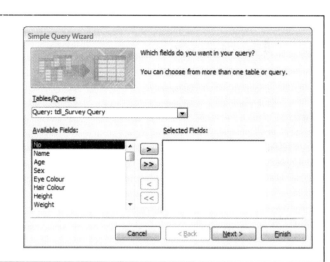

Simple Query Wizard

- Check to see that all the fields appear in the box under Selected Fields:.
- Click **Next >** to continue.

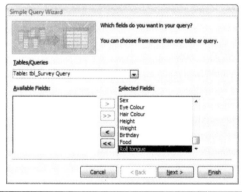

- Select
  - ◉ Detail (shows every field of every record)
- Click **Next >** to continue.

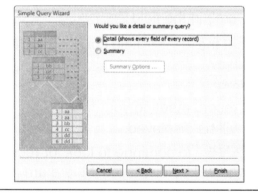

Final step

- You will still see all of the data as in Datasheet view, but now you are ready to select only relevant records. Use the default query name tbl_Survey Query for the question What title do you want for your query?
- You can change the query design later on.
- Select Open the query to view information.
- Click **Finish** to view the information.
- You will get all the data in the format of a spreadsheet.

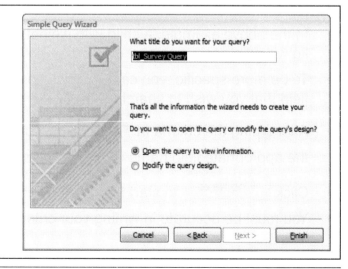

View data

- The result actually included all the records because we did not set any **criteria** on the query.
- Once the criteria is set, the result will show only the relevant records.

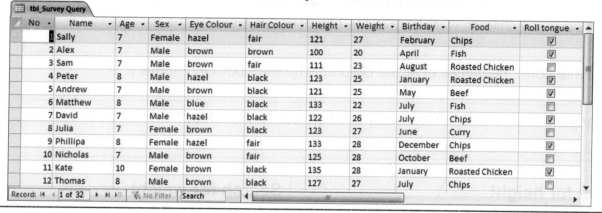

Criteria

- Click 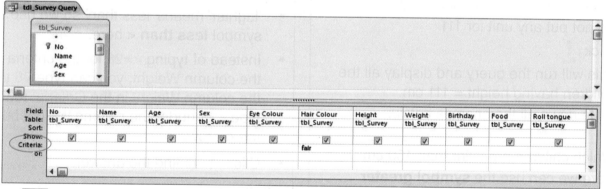 View to go to the Design view of the query. If you have trouble getting to Design view, right click tdl_Survey Query in the navigation panel and then click Design view.

- In the row **Criteria:**, under the header Hair Colour , type fair.

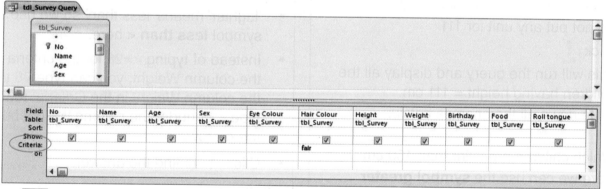

- Click Run .
- A list of the data for those with **fair hair colour** will be displayed.
- The total number of such records is shown at the bottom.

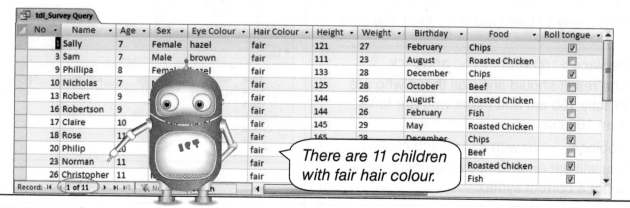

There are 11 children with fair hair colour.

4.7 Queries and search

More queries

- Click 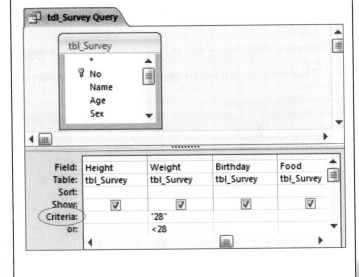. Delete the criteria fair under the Hair colour column.
- Type February in the criteria under Birthday and click ![Run].
  - How many children were born in the month of February?

    _____

  - Write down the names of all the children who were born in February.

    _____

- Change February to May. How many children were born in May?

    _____

Search for height

- Which children are 111 cm tall?
- To find the answer, we must first identify the criteria.
- The criteria is **height = 111 cm**.
- Click ![design] to change to the query design mode.
- Type 111 for criteria under Height.
- Do not put any unit for 111.
- Click ![Run].
- This will run the query and display all the children having height = 111 cm.
- Write down all their names below:

    _____

- Which children are taller than 160 cm?
- Here we can use the **symbol greater than >** for 'taller'.
- Click ![design] to change to the design mode again.
- Replace 111 with >160 and click ![Run].
- How many of them are taller than 160 cm?

    _____

- Replace >160 with >=160 and click ![Run].
- The result should show all those who are exactly 160 cm and those who are taller than 160 cm.
- Replace >=160 with =>160 and click ![Run].
- You will get an error message because => is not a correct syntax.

Search for weight

- Click ![design] to change to the query design mode.
- Hassan's weight is 28 kg.
- Find out how many of the children are lighter than **or** the same weight as Hassan.
- First identify the criteria.
- 'Lighter' means 'less than', so we use the symbol **less than <** here.
- Instead of typing <=28 for the criteria under the column Weight, you can type 28 under the column Weight in the Criteria: row and type <28 under the column Weight but in the or: row.
- Click ![Run] to find the answer.

Search for food

- Is your favourite food on the list?
- Click  to change to the query design mode.
- Search for others who like the same food as you.
- Find out how many children like chips or fish.

  _____

- How many of the children like curry or beef?

  _____

Hair

- These are the colours of the hair of the children in this survey.

  black   blonde   brown

  dark brown   fair   red

- Find out how many children have black hair, brown hair and dark brown hair.

Putting two searches together

- How many children are 144 cm tall?

  _____

- How many children weigh 26 kg?

  _____

- How many children are 144 cm tall and weigh 26 kg?

  - Click  to change to the query design mode.
  - Type 144 for criteria under Height.
  - Type 26 for criteria under Weight.
  - Click !.
    Run
  - Save the query as QHtWt.

  _____

Make up other searches

- How many children with blonde hair also have brown eyes?

  _____

- Save your query as query2.
- Who are the children that were born in July and can roll their tongues?

  _____

- Save your query as query3.

- Do any children with black hair also have blue eyes?

  _____

- Save your query as query4.

For Yes/No field, you only have to type YES or NO!

4.8 Search and sorting

Return the coat

- Find out who lost a coat.

- A coat was found.
- In the pocket the teacher found:
  - An ice cream wrapper.
  - A birthday card posted in May.
  - A girl's hair band.
- Create a query to find out who lost her coat by identifying the clues found by the teacher.
- 'An ice cream wrapper' indicates the owner likes to eat ice cream.
- 'A birthday card posted in May' indicates that the owner's birthday is in May.
- 'A girl's hair band' indicates the owner is a girl.
- Based on these criteria, find out who lost a coat.
- Save your query as FindCoat.

Return the shirt

- Find out who lost a shirt.
  - It had curry on it.
  - In the pocket was a star sign chart for December.

My favourite food is curry!

- Identify the criteria.
- 'It had curry on it' indicates the owner's favourite food is

_____

- 'a star sign chart for December' indicates that the birthday of the owner is in

_____

- Save your query as FindShirt.
- Run the query and identify the owner:

_____

Sort the records

- Open the file survey again.
- Open the table tbl_Survey.
- Place the mouse pointer on any of the names.
- Click on Home tab.

- In the Sort & Filter group click A↓Z.
- When you look through the records now, they are in alphabetical order: Alex, Andrew, Betty, Catherine etc.

I did the sorting by clicking the icon A↓Z.

Sort the records for age

- Open the file survey.
- Open the table tbl_Survey.
- Place the mouse pointer in any cell under Age.
- Click . This will sort the records by age in ascending order.

    _____ is the youngest at 7 years old.

- Click [Z A↓] while the mouse pointer is still in one of the cells under Age. This will sort the records in descending order.

    _____ is the eldest at 11 years old.

Sort by height and weight

- Sort the records by height in descending order.
- Click on any cell in the Height column.
- Click [A Z↓].
- What can you say about the person at the top of the table?

    _____ is the tallest at _____ cm.

- Are there any children with the same height?

    _____

- Sort the records by weight in descending order.
- Click on any cell in the Weight column.
- Click [A Z↓].
- What can you say about the person at the top of the table?

    _____ is the heaviest at _____ kg.

- Are there any children with the same weight?

    _____

Interpretation

- The following are some interpretations of the data after the sorting. Say whether each statement is **True** or **False**.

    ○ Rose is as tall **and** as heavy as Chong. (True/False)

    ○ Alex is shortest of all and he is also the lightest among the group. (True/False)

    ○ Christopher is taller but lighter than Jenny. (True/False)

    ○ The tallest boy is also the eldest of all. (True/False)

- Sort the records by Food.
- Are all the students who like to eat beef born in the same month?

    _____

- Sort the records by Birthday.
- What is the most popular food for the students born in December?

    _____

- What is the most common colour of hair? Sort the appropriate column to find out.

    _____

4.10 Interpretation of data

Interpret data

- The query below helps to answer the question: 'Who are the girls who like to eat roasted chicken?'

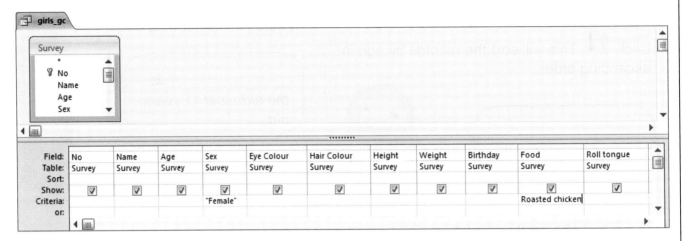

- The result shows that Kate, Claire and Siti are the girls who like to eat roasted chicken.

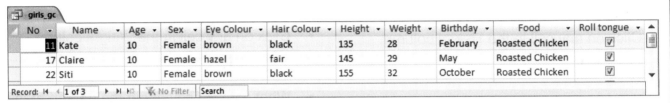

- From the results above, we can also obtain other relevant information:
  - All the three girls are 10 years old.
  - All the three girls can roll their tongues.
  - Two of the girls have black hair.
  - The heights of the three girls are all above 130 cm.

Using query

- Use **query** to find out how many boys (males) were born in January **or** September.
- Save your query as boys_JS.
- From the searched result, write down 2 more observations about the data.

_____

_____

- Use **query** to find out how many children weighing between 28 kg and 35 kg have brown eyes. (Hint: type >27 and <36 for criteria under Weight.)
- Save your query as wt_range.
- From the searched result, write down 2 more observations about the data.

_____

_____

Optional extension and challenge activities

Module 4 – Exploring Databases

Challenge 1

Do boys or girls most like to watch TV?

Do boys or girls most like to play sport?

Do boys or girls most like to make things?

Do boys or girls most like to read?

- Create a database to answer these questions, using data supplied by your friends or family.

Challenge 2

- Create a database to record the type and number of birds seen near the school.
- Record if they hop or walk.
- Record whether they like to eat seeds or insects. (You could use a search engine to check this).
- Use the database to see what is the most common bird in the area and what it likes to eat.
- Do most of these birds prefer to hop or walk on the ground?

Optional extension and challenge activities

Challenge 3

Do people with big feet have long hands?

Do people with big hands have a wider hand span?

- Measure the foot length and hand length and hand span of your friends.
- Create records which show this data.
- Sort the records to help answer these questions.